I Remember Samson

Darlene Winter

ISBN 978-1-61225-125-7

Published by Mirror Publishing
Milwaukee, WI 53214
www.pagesofwonder.com

Printed in the USA.

This book is being dedicated to the men and women who work with the primates at the Milwaukee County Zoo, Milwaukee, WI. All proceeds from this book will be given to The Great Ape Heart Project at The Milwaukee County Zoo

INTRODUCTION

Not a day goes by at The Milwaukee County Zoo that a staff member or a volunteer doesn't hear a visitor say, "I remember Samson." He was as well known as Fonzie, LaVerne and Shirley, and even Milwaukee's politicians. Many people at that time came to the zoo just to see Samson.

His reputation extended far beyond the state of Wisconsin. Many felt he was the largest gorilla in captivity. It was reported that a story about him appeared in a Bankok newspaper and that his picture was exhibited in a primate center in Japan. He had even been mentioned in several books about gorillas. Samson became an ambassador not only for the zoo, but for gorillas in general, since at that time there were only a few in captivity and little was known about them.

I felt, however, that a story of Samson needed to be expanded somewhat to incorporate information on zoos and the development and evaluation of gorillas in captivity.

Chapter 1

Ancient Times

The oldest known zoological collection was discovered in 2009 at an archeological dig in Egypt. It was believed to be from around 3500 BC and included such exotic animals as hippos, elephants, baboons, and wildcats. In the 2nd century, BCE, the Chinese Empress Tanki had a house built for her deer and King Wen of Zhou had a 1,500 acre zoo. Other well-known animal collectors were King Solomon and King Nebuchadnezzar of Babylonia. By the 4th century, BCE, zoos existed in most Greek city states. Alexander the Great sent back animals he found on his military expeditions. Roman emperors kept private collections of animals for study or use in the arena, where many animals died.

Medieval Times

Henry I of England kept a collection of animals at his palace in Woodstock which included lions, leopards, and camels. The most prominent collection was in the Tower of London, created as early as 1204 by King John I. Henry III received, as a wedding gift in 1235, three leopards from Fredrick II Holy Roman Emperor. In 1264, the animals were moved to the Bulwark, renamed the Lion Tower near the western entrance to the tower. It was opened to the public during the reign of Elizabeth I in the 16th century. During the 18th century, the price of admission was three half-pence or a cat or dog for feeding the lions. The animals were moved to the London Zoo when it opened.

Later Years

The London Zoo opened in 1828 and at first called itself a menagerie or "zoological garden," short for "Gardens and menagerie of the Zoological Society of London." The abbreviation "zoo" first appeared in print in the United Kingdom around 1847.

The oldest existing zoo is the Vienna Zoo in Austria and was opened to the public in 1754. In 1859, a charter establishing the Zoological Society of Philadelphia Zoo was confirmed but the zoo did not actually open to the public until July 1, 1874. The delay was due to the civil war. Central Park in New York had a menagerie and, in 1864, it received a charter confirmation as a zoo and opened to the public that same year.

Zoos began to spring up all over the world and, in 1924, the Association of Zoos and Aquariums (AZA) (formerly known as American Association of Zoological Parks and Aquariums) was formed as an affiliate of the American Institute of Park Executives. In January 1972 it became an independent association.

In 1970, ecology emerged as a matter of public interest and a few zoos in the U.S., together with the AZA, decided to make conservation its highest priority. Many zoos stopped having their animals perform tricks for visitors.

Human Exhibits

In 1904, a Congolese Mbuti pygmy named Ota Benga was purchased from slave traders who had attacked his village, killing his wife and two children. Samuel Phillips, employed by the Louisiana Purchase Exposition, had negotiated Ota's release and Ota was featured in an anthropology display for the Louisiana Exhibition. After about two years of travel, Ota was caged at the Bronx Zoo where he was exhibited in the monkey house as part of a display intended to promote concepts of human evolution and scientific racism. Ota would carry an orangutan around the cage like a father. After repeated protests from local clergy, the mayor finally had Ota released. However, he was released to be institutionalized where he died at the age of 32.

Human beings were also displayed in cages during the 1931 Paris Colonial Exposition and as late as 1958 in a "Congolese village" display at Expo '58 in Brussels.

Zoo Accreditation

Accreditation means official recognition and approval of a zoo or aquarium obtained after completion of a detailed application and a multi-day on-site inspection by a team of experts from around the country. Only those zoos and aquariums that meet their high standards can become members of AZA.

The benefits of an accreditation develops the public's confidence in the zoo or aquarium knowing that the institution meets or exceeds current professional standards. The accreditation provides a publicly recognized badge signifying excellence in, and commitment to, such things as animal care, conservation, education, and distinguishes AZA-accredited zoos and aquariums from "roadside zoos." It also allows the institution to participate in animal exchanges with other AZA institutions and to collaborate with other AZA colleagues in the valuable exchange of information.

Chapter 2

The Washington Park Zoo

In 1892, Milwaukee officials decided they wanted to create a zoo. It was named West Park Zoo and began with 8 deer donated by Louis Auer and Col. Gustave Pabst.

Later, an eagle was donated by Louis Lotz, a druggist. In 1899, the first structure was built to house the herbivore animals.

Edward H. Bean, first director of the zoo, and his friend Chili.

On September 29, 1900, the name was changed to the Washington Park Zoo and in 1906, Edward Bean became the first zoo director until 1927. Ed's philosophy was not to have a great number of individual species but to exhibit as great a number of species as was consistent with their good care and companionship. That's why when Ed started in 1906, the zoo had 75 animals and when he left, the zoo had 800 animals.

In 1919, a polar bear was born at the zoo, which was the first cub born in captivity in North America. Congratulations came from all over the world, putting Washington Park Zoo "on the map."

In 1927, an innovation of considerable scientific interest and public popularity took place. Green lights were installed to achieve a moonlight effect in the zoo and the public could now see wildlife at night.

Throughout the 1930s, the most popular primate at the zoo was the chimpanzee named Mary Lou. She would dine at 4 p.m. each day, sitting at a table using a knife, fork, and spoon. She would mimic and entertain the zoo crowd. While wearing a dress and hat, she would visit the downtown Gimbels store with her keeper.

In 1937, it became evident that the zoo was deteriorating. Exhibit lighting was inadequate as bars and other ironwork needed repair. Also, the zoo had no room to expand the 23 acres it then occupied. The zoo was now under the jurisdiction of Milwaukee County and in order for the zoo to be moved to larger quarters where there would still be ample space to expand further, it was necessary for the boundary of Milwaukee's city limits to be expanded so that the land could then be purchased for the zoo. Such an expansion was complete and that is why Milwaukee County extends out almost like a finger in between West Allis and Wauwatosa, so that the zoo could remain part of the Milwaukee County park system.

In 1947, George Speidel became zoo director until 1978. He received his training from Edward Bean, which is not surprising since Ed was George's father-in-law. George believed in hands-on experience as the best teacher. His dream was a zoo that showed animals in a realistic setting with no bars and fences. He wanted animals to be separated

by wide moats so visitors could see animals in panorama. He was, therefore, greatly responsible for the way the zoo exhibits are today.

Pabst Brewing Company donated $10,000 to purchase a couple of giant pandas from China for the zoo. However, China closed its borders and it was impossible to get any pandas. It was decided, therefore, to use the money to purchase a couple of gorillas.

Chapter 3

In the 1940s, George contacted an animal broker in New York requesting two young gorillas for the zoo. At that time, to get any young animal meant contacting an animal broker who would contact a company in Africa, or whatever appropriate region, and negotiate for the animals needed. Capturing gorillas probably consisted of having men dig a pit or construct nets and then having men called "beaters" make loud noises, driving the animals to the pit or nets. Once captured, the adults were probably killed so the young could be easily handled without danger to the men.

It was now May 1950 and George flew to New York to study the six young gorillas the broker had for sale. He was going to pick out two for the zoo. After George studied them for a while, he selected the two that, in his opinion, were the brightest, liveliest, and healthiest of the lot. They had been acquired from the then French Cameroun in West Africa. Samson and Sambo were the names given them by the broker before George acquired them and even after the zoo ran a naming contest, it was decided that they would keep their original names. While their exact age was not known, it was believed that Sambo was roughly about a year old and weighed 15 pounds. Samson was believed to be a little younger, weighing in at just 12.5 pounds.

Sambo and Samson were Western Lowland Gorillas, which are a sub-species of gorillas and are the species most found in zoos worldwide. There are approximately 340 gorillas in North American zoos. They are the smaller of the gorillas and the easiest to keep in captivity. If you check various sources and search gorillas' physical characteristics, you'll see that the male Western Lowland Gorilla is suppose to weigh about 374 lbs. And even though animals do weigh more in captivity, I don't think anyone could have guessed that Samson would get as big as he did.

In October 1950, George boarded the plane in New York with two additional passengers that no one suspected were gorillas. They slept most of the way, being wakened briefly for a bottle of milk. George carried them off the plane and was welcomed by news reporters and an excited public. They were then introduced to Mrs. Edith Scott, the zoo matron who was to be in charge of them during their infancy.

A special exhibit had been prepared that somewhat resembled a nursery. However, Samson and Sambo both arrived at the zoo with pneumonia and it was touch and go as to whether they would survive. Edith, along with other staff, worked around the clock to save them. They overcame the pneumonia and began to adjust to their new life.

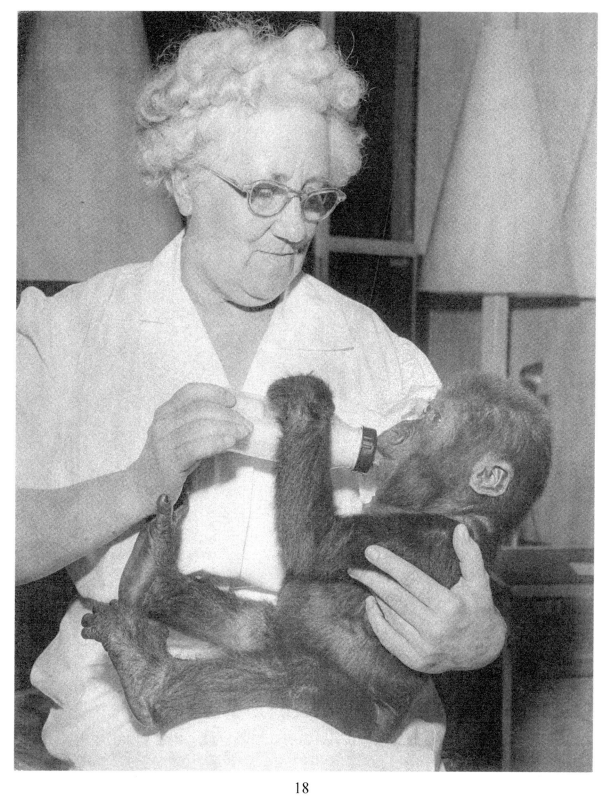

Their day started at 8 a.m. when Edith would give them formula consisting of condensed milk, water, dextrose syrup, and cereal fortified with wheat germ oil and calcium. This would be the first of three such feedings. She originally tried to feed them with a spoon but they were afraid of it. Eventually they learned to accept it. In addition, twice a day they were given all the fruit and raw vegetables they could eat. Pineapple proved to be their favorite. Since the zoo had never had gorillas before, it was hit or miss as to what to feed them. You experiment just as you would with a young child. If they eat it, great. If they throw it at you or spit it up, that's a food you check off the list.

Mrs. Scott spent her entire day with the gorillas and visitors could watch her rocking them and cuddling them. During the early years, gorillas gain about 3 lbs. a month. Sambo was 3 lbs. heavier than Samson and when they developed enough to climb and play, they had to be separated some times because Sambo was too big, powerful, and rough for little Samson.

The matronly care lasted until they were about 4 years old.

Their notoriety began at an early age. In 1955, Marlin Perkins from the television show *Zoo Parade* came to Milwaukee to film an episode and to visit the gorillas at the Washington Park Zoo. He talked about their age, their weight, what their future weight would be, and even got to feed them, through the bars, of course.

As mentioned earlier, the exhibits at the Washington Park Zoo were very small, stark, and drab. So when it came to designing a new gorilla exhibit at the new location, George wanted a state-of-the-art exhibit. He wanted brightness, so green tiles were used on the walls, plenty of light, and a large space. It contained a square water basin and a shelf or landing on either side of the exhibit for the gorillas to sit or lie down. There were also a couple of tires hanging by ropes from the ceiling for them to play with and one that they could throw around. The exhibit was completely tiled and the floor slanted slightly with an automatic flushing system to help maintain sanitation. There was also a scale put in the exhibit so the public could see how much the gorillas weighed. Sambo and Samson were now approximately 10 years old when they were moved to the new zoo location. Just one month after the move, Sambo died. It was discovered that he died of tuberculosis, which he presumably contracted at the old zoo location where the gorillas were more exposed to the public. Samson was put on antibiotics immediately just as a precaution. Thank goodness he never contracted the disease. It was decided, however, that glass would be installed on the new exhibit and the air system would be separate from the public's to ensure that Samson would not contract any diseases. The glass was actually a sheet of glass about ¼ inch thick surrounded on each side by ¼ inch plexiglass. The plexiglass on the inside of the exhibit was designed to emit a slight electric shock if Samson were to touch it. You can still see the exhibit today, minus the big tires, the scale, and the green tiles. The Colobus monkeys now reside there.

Chapter 4

After Sambo died, Samson was alone. When Sam LaMalfa began working at the zoo in 1964, he worked with all of the primates. However, he knew that there was something special about Samson. Sam also knew how to work with the primates and how to gain their trust. With Samson, Sam would talk slow and low. Even though Samson may not have understood every word Sam said, repetition of some words had meaning. It's like working with your dog or even your cat. They do recognize certain words and what is then expected of them. Sam knew that gorillas were very social animals and he realized too, that for Samson to be alone was not good for him, so Sam spent every free minute he could with Samson. Samson came to trust Sam completely as a friend and someone who meant him no harm and only wanted to take care of him. Samson was alone for 16 years.

The zoo added two baby gorillas in April 1960 by the names of Tanga and Terra. Tanga, the male, and Terra, the female, grew up together. They didn't have contact with Samson. They had been basically hand raised together although they were not related. Having been raised by humans and imprinted on humans, they forgot how to be gorillas. Tanga became frustrated as he became an adult and didn't know what to do. He began to slap Terra around so Sam had to separate them permanently.

When the zoo began to get exotic animals, much of what they knew about their care came from whatever written material was available, which, at that time, was very little or from other keepers at other zoos. Sometimes it was just plain trial and error.

When Sam would put Samson's food on the scale, you'd see a loaf of bread, fruits, vegetables, and commercially prepared primate biscuits. Obviously many of these items were not found in the jungles of Africa.

Samson
loved
it all.

So much, in fact, that in 1970, Samson weighed 652 lbs.

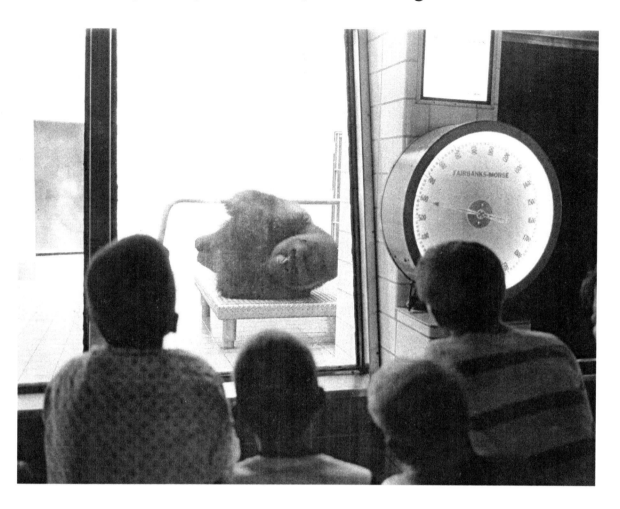

Even though Samson had a big frame, Sam knew that this much weight was not good for him.

Sam put Samson on a diet. Now anyone who has gone on a diet knows how hard it can be and how cranky you can become not being able to eat all the things you like. So, how do you put a 652 lb. gorilla on a diet? Sam did it slowly. He would withhold a banana here or a few slices of bread there and eventually after about a year and a half, Samson got down to 532 lbs. which was a comfortable weight for a male gorilla his size.

Sam talked to George about putting Terra in with Samson. At first George was not in favor of the idea. With Samson being such a big guy and Terra being much smaller, George was afraid Terra would get hurt. Eventually George agreed to unite the two and even had hopes that they might produce a baby.

In the spring of 1975, two sections of a holding area downstairs, off exhibit, were renovated with a door built between the two sections, with a smaller door inside it that would slide. Because Terra, now 16 years old, was an average size female, and Samson was much bigger, the small door was used to Sam's advantage. Terra could fit through the small door and Samson couldn't, so she could escape if necessary. Then Sam would be able to slide the door closed and they would be separated from each other.

After she was moved into the cage, she was given a chance to adjust to it for a few weeks. When Sam first left everything open so Samson could see her, Sam said the expression on Samson's face was priceless. It was like, "Oh, my gosh, what is that sharing my bedroom?"

When the two first went on exhibit together, they ran around the platform scale a few times and then just stopped and looked at each other. It was a big media event.

For the next week, Sam would feed Samson on the left side of the exhibit and the other keepers would feed Terra on the right. But Samson started getting upset because he didn't want to share. Sam decided that they could not be fed together so, from then on, Terra was fed downstairs and Samson upstairs. When they were done eating ,Terra would be put upstairs again. They lived this way for more than 4 years.

The hope that a Baby Samson would be born, however, did not happen. Samson too, had been imprinted by humans and, like Tanga, Samson had no idea what to do or the inclination to do anything. It was thankful that he did not exhibit Tanga's frustration toward Terra,

because given his size, it could have been brutal. However, the press seemed to find the whole affair, or should I say lack of an affair, quite hilarious. Samson was called a Don Yawn and the press actually wrote a story that Samson and Terra were getting a divorce and created a fake interview with Terra about how she felt.

I'm sure the public got a kick out of it at the time. Looking back now, it just goes to show how little was known about the gorilla personality. This also shows the importance of socializing gorillas at an early age to create a normal gorilla group.

It was decided that Terra needed a new mate so Sam took her to the Lincoln Park Zoo in Chicago in 1979. Terra was introduced to Frank the gorilla and it was love at first sight. In 1981, she gave birth to Mandara. However, she was unable to care for the baby either because of inexperience or poor milk quality. Mandara needed 24-

hour care for several months so she was brought back to Milwaukee and the Mandara Moms, consisting of trained volunteers, took care of her. Mandara eventually went to the National Zoo in Washington, D.C. where she became a great mom and had several babies.

After Terra left, the public may have thought that Samson was mad or sad because he always looked like that. What some people may not know is that gorillas (primates) cannot move their cheek muscles, so they cannot smile. They do, however, have very pliable lips. I'm sure you've seen one of them pull his lower or upper lip way out so they can look at it. Samson was able to make his lips protrude through the bars every morning so he could have his energy drink.

Since Samson was alone again, he turned to Sam for his companionship. Samson thought of Sam as belonging to him.

Some people have said to Sam, "You were so close to Samson, how come you never went in with him?"

Sam would say, "If I ever went in with him, he would never let me leave."

Samson was very jealous of anyone who came near Sam. Sometimes it was necessary for Sam to being someone behind the exhibit to see Samson. It could have been a newspaper reporter or a visiting VIP. But no matter who it was, when Sam would open the door and Samson would see that Sam was not alone, he would start to pound his chest and make hooting sounds and even run and hit the other door. All this was a big bluff to scare the intruder away from Sam.

Sam and Samson even played games when Samson was in his night quarters. Samson was given burlap bags to play with. One night Sam saw a strip of burlap partially sticking out of Samson's cage. Sam started to pull it slowly, grunting and groaning as if the piece weighed a ton. Samson sat quietly and watched this until the piece of burlap was almost out of the cage. Then Samson grabbed it. He would shake his head and hit his chest in a playful manner. When Samson pulled the burlap into the cage, Sam would then tell Samson, "Ok, you win." Samson would push the burlap out again and Sam would pick up the end and begin to pull it again. Samson would let it go so far and then he would stop it. The two would play this game until Sam had to leave to resume other duties.

At one point, Samson became ill. He had to get medicine at least three times a day. When Sam called Samson over to get the medicine for the first time, Samson took one whiff of it and backed away. He didn't like the smell. So Sam decided to try mixing the medicine with yogurt and fresh fruit. He then tried to spoon feed Samson the mixture. Samson enjoyed it and this went on for a couple of days. One day while Sam was feeding him, Samson bit down on the spoon and took off with it. Sam very quietly and slowly told Samson to bring it back. Samson ignored his request. Sam asked a little louder and in a sterner voice. Again no response. Sam's voice became louder and by his tone Samson could tell he was not kidding around. So Samson began to push the spoon toward the door. Sam wanted Samson to hand him the spoon because he felt Samson needed to respect Sam's authority. Sam continued to ask for the spoon and Samson just kept pushing it closer. Finally the spoon was at the door but Samson still would not pick it up. Sam had a banana in his back pocket so he took it out and Samson handed Sam the spoon for the banana. Sam got him to pick up the spoon but Samson got the last laugh, because after that, Sam always had to carry a banana.

Sam believed that on some level Samson knew he was a king, or at least the center of attention. Not a day went by that he didn't have an audience three to four rows deep of people who had come to see him.

He played his audience. He would survey the crowd and when he knew it was just the right time, he would begin his show. He would start out with some quiet hooting. He would let it build louder and louder until he would take off unexpectedly toward the front of the exhibit and hit the glass. The audience would scatter. But as frightened as they were, they would always come back to see if he would do it again. And even though they knew that eventually he would, he would always catch them off guard and they would scatter again. Sam believed that Samson was acting out his role as leader of a gorilla troop. He realized soon enough that the public's reaction to his hitting the window was his way of showing power and control. Males display charging, beating of the chest, and uprooting their surroundings in order to convey the message, "I'm in charge." This behavior is also used to scare predators away like leopards that may be in pursuit of a baby gorilla for dinner.

Some people have wondered how many times he broke the glass. Some people may even believe that he actually escaped at least once. However, Samson only cracked the glass 4 times. The glass had plexiglass on either side so, even though the glass was cracked, you could run you hand over it and it would still be smooth to the touch. Samson never did break out of his exhibit and even if he had, like most animals on exhibit, he would have been scared and probably would have tried to get back into his exhibit because that was home. The majority of the animals today at the Milwaukee County Zoo were born in zoos and are very comfortable with the zoo routine. They wouldn't have any idea what to do if they were free.

Chapter 5

On November 27, 1981, while in the middle of his meal, Samson fell over dead. The keepers went into the exhibit but there was nothing they could have done. His death resounded around the zoo immediately and staff and visitors alike began to cry. The switchboard operator had the horrible task of calling Sam at home to tell him the news. Sam had been off for the Thanksgiving weekend. The operator was crying so hard when she told Sam that at first he could not understand what she was saying. But as the message became clearer, the shock hit him. He had just lost his friend. Sam rushed to the zoo almost hoping that perhaps there had been a mistake or that Samson was playing some new game. But when he saw him, there was no doubt.

A necropsy was performed and it showed that Samson had actually had five heart attacks prior to the one that killed him, but no one knew. He was 32 years old. Samson was put into a freezer and, unfortunately, his skin developed probable freezer burn so that when it was decided that Samson would go to Milwaukee's Public Museum, he was not able to be mounted as his earlier companion Sambo had been. Therefore, his skeleton became one of their exhibits.

In 2006, a new museum director learned that he had the famous Samson in his collection of exhibits. He felt that Samson needed to be brought back to life, so-to-speak, so he asked staff member Wendy Christensen-Senk to work on this project. Wendy worked closely with Sam, who provided many photos of Samson in different poses. These, together with the death mask made of Samson, plus the body measurements that were taken at the time of his death, proved invaluable in Wendy's re-creation of Samson.

Today the re-creation of Samson stands in a glass exhibit at the top of the main stairway of the museum. Wendy did such a fantastic job that Samson almost looks alive and you'd expect him again to hit the glass at any moment.

Samson has never been forgotten. Every January since 1980, Samson Stomp is held at the zoo. It is a walk/run event where participants either walk or run a 5K, 2 mile, 1 mile, or ¼ mile route around the zoo and all the monies provide for all the animals in the zoo.

Chapter 6

The practice of capturing wild animals for zoos was stopped by The Endangered Species Conservation Act, which was passed in December 1969. It amended the original law to provide additional protection to species in danger of "worldwide extinction" by prohibiting their importation and subsequent sale in the U.S.

President Nixon, however, felt the conservation efforts were inadequate and asked the 93rd Congress to pass a more comprehensive plan, which they did. The Endangered Species Act was signed by President Nixon in 1973.

In 1981, the Species Survival Program (SSP) was started to manage and conserve a select threatened or endangered species population with the cooperation of AZA. SSP species are often flagship species, well known animals which create strong feelings in the public for the preservation and protection of the wild populations and their habitats, gorillas among them. Currently there are more than 300 SSP programs. Each SSP program is responsible for developing a Population Analysis & Breeding and Transfer Plan that manages and recommends zoo populations of these species which ensures the sustainability of healthy, genetically diverse and varied populations.

Today, no animals are taken from the wild unless it is to prevent them from becoming totally extinct. Then reproduction is encouraged to increase their numbers and hopefully re-introduce them into the wild.

Chapter 7

There is no doubt that the research provided by the men and women who choose to go into the jungles to study primates, is invaluable. The zoo learned that gorillas are very social and actually thrive in the company of others. The zoo will never again have a lone gorilla like Samson.

The zoo keepers today are also working to make sure that the primates learn from each other on how to be primates. Interaction with humans are kept to a minimum.

A nutritionist now controls their diets to make sure they maintain a healthy weight. No more bread and sweets except for an occasional yogurt, which is a treat. A veterinarian and a dentist also maintain their health. A state-of-the-art health facility was built in 2003 on the zoo grounds so that if an animal needs medical care, a complete health and dental examination can also be done while the animal is under anesthesia.

It's actually healthier for the primate if they don't have to be anesthetized for routine checkups so that is why the keepers work with them so they can be examined through the bars. They get the primates to open their mouths so the keeper can see their teeth and the keepers get them to present their hands so that blood can be taken. Of course, the primate will be given a treat which is their motivation to comply.

The zoo keepers, together with a cardiologist, have managed to get the gorillas and bonobos to stand quietly against the bars so an ultrasound examination can be performed. The Milwaukee County Zoo was the first to be able to accomplish this with their primates.

Even though the threat of the apes catching a cold, flu, or pneumonia still exists, the zoo no longer keeps them totally confined behind glass enclosures. Many of the primates today have an outside exhibit that is filled with trees, grass, and objects to stimulate their minds and bodies.

Chapter 8

Had the zoo keepers known then what they know today, Samson's life would have been very different. He would have been paired with another gorilla right after Sambo died and human contact would have been kept to a minimum. He would have had an indoor exhibit that gave him the opportunity to get away from the public's view, if he wished to do so.

He would have eaten better, stayed slimmer, and had access to the outside.

He also would have had the advantage of the ultrasound procedure being performed today on the primates, which possibly could have detected any heart problems earlier. He most likely would have lived longer than his 32 years and we might have been lucky enough to have some of his offspring at the zoo today.

Each and every day we are all learning more and more about the animals in the zoo and together with the research that continues in the wild, we will hopefully learn how to coexist and protect these animals from extinction.

We may not all be zoo keepers or animal researchers, but we all can and should make it our responsibility to take a part in conservation. Every one of us doing the most simplest of things, such as recycling or being conscientious about the products we purchase, CAN make a difference.

Acknowledgements

I have to, of course, thank Sam LaMalfa, Samson's keeper and friend. This book would probably never have been written without his input and pictures. A special thank you also has to be given to Robert M. Davis, DVM, Zoological Society President/CEO of the Milwaukee County Zoo, without whose support would not have made this book possible.

I must thank the Milwaukee Journal/Sentinel for their generous donation of the pictures included in this book. I must also thank Allan Y. Scott for the pictures he generously allowed us to use. Pictures were also contributed by the Milwaukee County Department of Parks, Recreation and Culture, the Milwaukee County Zoological Gardens, Tom Parkes, Wendy Christensen-Senk, the Milwaukee Public Museum, as well as several pictures which were photographed by persons unknown.

A special thanks also goes to Mary Kazmierczak and the Milwaukee County Zoo's Creative Department for preparing the pictures for publication. I would like to thank other zoo staff and volunteers whose support and belief in this project helped make it possible for me to finish.

CPSIA information can be obtained at www.ICGtesting.com
Printed in the USA
LVOW091241110512

281305LV00003B/1/P